THE PARANORMAL THROUGHOUT HISTORY

ESP CASES

IN HISTORY

ANITA CROY

rosen publishing's
rosen
central

New York

Published in 2020 by The Rosen Publishing Group, Inc.
29 East 21st Street
New York, NY 10010

First Edition

Produced for Rosen by Calcium Creative Ltd
Editors for Calcium: Sarah Eason and Harriet McGregor
Designer: Paul Myerscough and Jessica Moon
Picture researcher: Rachel Blount

Photo credits: Cover: Shutterstock: N_defender; Inside: Library of Congress: Wright, George Hand: p. 27; Shutterstock: AlexHliv: p. 18; Anna Andersson Fotografi: p. 33b; BlackMac: p. 8; Andrea Danti: pp. 4-5t; Elgreko: p. 6; Everett Collection: p. 26; Everett Historical: pp. 11b, 16; Foto011: pp. 40-41; Gilmanshin: p. 7; Fer Gregory: p. 25; Inked Pixels: pp. 1, 5r; Jorisvo: pp. 12, 15; Martina Kieselbach: p. 20; Linas T: p. 43; PRESSLAB: p. 38; Jana Rudt: pp. 10-11t; Silvaner: p. 13; Ken Tannenbaum: pp. 36-37; TAW4: pp. 3, 32-33; Wikimedia Commons: pp. 17, 29, 31, 34-35; Vincenzo Camuccini/Ribberlinp: p. 9; Pfc. James Cox: p. 42; Walt Cisco, Dallas Morning News: p. 35r; Unattributed; based on the depiction from a mechanical glass slide by T. M. McAllister of New York, c1865-75: p. 28; Paul Mellon Collection in the Yale Center for British Art: p. 19; Neznámý: p. 30; Open Media Ltd: p. 39; Matthew Paris: p. 14; Rama: p. 21; Carl Fredric von Breda: p. 22; Albert von Schrenck-Notzing: p. 24.

Cataloging-in-Publication Data

Names: Croy, Anita.
Title: ESP cases in history / Anita Croy.
Description: New York : Rosen Central, 2020. | Series: The paranormal throughout history | Includes glossary and index.
Identifiers: ISBN 9781725346611 (pbk.) | ISBN 9781725346550 (library bound)
Subjects: LCSH: Extrasensory perception—Juvenile literature.
Classification: LCC BF1321.C79 2020 | DDC 133.8—dc23

Cover: Some people claim that tools such as crystal balls help them "see" beyond the present to foretell the future.

CONTENTS

CHAPTER 1
ANCIENT SEERS

Extra sensory perception, or ESP, is a phrase that describes people's ability to experience something without using their physical senses. The five senses are hearing, sight, touch, smell, and taste. ESP is sometimes called the sixth sense. It is impossible to define it accurately, because it is something that exists beyond the ordinary physical world. Many people insist that it exists—but others deny that there is any such thing.

Telepathy is the ability to tell what someone else is thinking without him or her speaking.

For people who believe in ESP, there are many different types of extra-sensory activity. One common kind of ESP is telepathy, which is being able to read another person's thoughts. The ability to see something happening in a different place is called clairvoyance, while being able to see into the future or the past is known as precognition or retrocognition. Some people claim they can "talk" to the dead, a skill called mediumship, while others say they can learn things about people or places from a single object. This is called psychometry.

For people who do not believe in ESP, it is easy to dismiss. There is no proof that it exists. Even people who do believe in ESP disagree about who possesses these abilities. Some say everyone is capable of ESP, but others believe that only a few people have the skills.

An Ancient Skill

ESP is as old as humankind. For thousands of years, people have told stories about events that seem to have been predicted by seers with the ability to tell the future. Many ancient peoples had special priests or magicians who claimed to be able to visit or contact a special place beyond the everyday world.

Some forms of ESP use crystal balls to predict the future.

Naming ESP

The phrase "extra sensory perception" was first used by the British explorer Sir Richard Burton in 1870. The term became much more widely known after 1934, when Joseph Banks Rhine, a science professor at Duke University, used it to describe what he admitted was indescribable. At the time, he was carrying out research on the paranormal, or things that are "beyond" normal.

THE GREEK ORACLES

In ancient Greece, some women were said to have the ability to communicate directly with the gods who controlled life on Earth. These women, or Sibyls, lived as priestesses called oracles in temples across Greece. Their job was to act as a go-between for the gods and the people who came to the temples to ask for advice. People who visited the oracle believed the gods could see into the future and predict coming events.

The most famous of all the Greek oracles was at the shrine of Apollo at Delphi. Apollo was the Greek god of the sun and the arts, and the chief god of the oracles. For almost 2,000 years, people visited the shrine to ask Apollo for advice. They spoke to the Sibyl in a cave, where she went into a trance, or dreamlike state, to talk to the god. The Sibyl's trance may have been caused naturally by gases coming into the cave through cracks in the rock.

The famous shrine of Apollo at Delphi was located on the slopes of a mountain called Parnassus.

Visit to the Sibyl

Before visitors could ask their questions, they had to pay a fee. Then they bathed and walked up the Sacred Way to the temple. They killed a sheep or goat as a sacrifice, and priests examined the animal's insides for omens, which were signs of what the gods were thinking. When the pilgrims finally reached the cave, they asked the Sibyl their questions. Sometimes, the Sibyl's answers were easy to understand, but most of the time they were like riddles with many meanings. The high priests of the shrine helped visitors try to figure out what the advice meant.

The messages passed on from Apollo by the oracle were famous for having more than one possible meaning.

The Delphic Oracle Speaks

In 480 BCE, the Greek city of Athens was under attack by invaders from Persia. The Athenians asked the oracle at Delphi for advice. The oracle told them to put their faith in wooden walls. Athens itself had stone walls, so the message was a mystery until the Athenians realized that their warships were made from wood—which were the "walls" that protected the city. They sent out their fleet and defeated the Persians at sea.

7

THE IDES OF MARCH

"Beware the Ides of March" is a line from a play by the English writer William Shakespeare about Julius Caesar, the first ruler of the huge Roman Empire. The play is based on the real events surrounding Caesar's death. A soothsayer, who is someone who can see the future, warns Caesar that he will die on the Ides of March, which in the Roman calendar was March 15, 44 BCE. Caesar ignores the prediction and carries on as normal. By the end of the day, he is dead.

ESP in Ancient Rome

The Romans were very superstitious people who believed in all sorts of ESP. They inherited many of their superstitions from the Greeks. Most Romans lived their daily lives observing superstitions and reading omens to try to tell the future. Before any important decision, Romans followed rituals and studied signs, such as the shape of a flock of birds in the sky, to try to tell what the future might bring.

Romans had altars to their household gods, whom they asked for signs about the best course of action to take.

Soothsayers

Soothsayers were important members of society. Families had their own soothsayers, whom they believed could talk to the gods and advise them how to live their lives according to the gods' wishes. Caesar was too proud to believe his soothsayer. He thought he was surrounded by friends, but in both Shakespeare's play and real life it was the men closest to him that killed him.

Julius Caesar was stabbed to death by people who believed he had too much power.

Ancient Wisdom

Different ancient cultures had different ways of "reading" the future. The Greeks were among many peoples who killed animals and then studied their insides to learn the gods' intentions. More than 3,000 years ago in China, priests of the Shang Dynasty carved questions about the future on animal bones. The bones were then heated until they cracked. The priests interpreted the patterns of the cracks to figure out what the future held.

SECOND SIGHT

Hundreds of years ago, the Gael people lived in the Highlands of Scotland. They believed that some people were able to see into the future. In their Gaelic language, they called this gift *"an da shealladh,"* which translates as two sights. Today, it is usually called second sight.

The Gaels were one of the Celtic peoples who lived in Scotland and Ireland. Celtic folk stories are full of accounts of people who could foresee events that later came true. These seers were also able to see things that other people could not see. Some were able to see the fairy kingdom, which was said to exist alongside the normal world but was invisible to most people.

People with second sight saw the highland landscape as being full of fairies and the spirits of the dead.

For the ancient Celts, second sight was a gift. Later in history, however, it was dangerous, especially for women. In the seventeenth century, for example, some women were thought to be witches because of their ability to predict events. For Christians, this was a sign that they were working with the devil. Women found guilty of being witches were often killed.

A Wartime Example

Some people still believe in second sight. During World War II (1939–1945), a Scottish officer was sailing in a convoy when he dreamed that the ship was bombed by a German plane. When he awoke, he told his superiors about his dream, including where the bomb would strike the ship. Soon after, the ship was bombed exactly as he had described. The officer had to convince his superiors that he was not a German spy.

Modern Second Sight

Other forms of second sight include being able to see people after they die and knowing about a person before meeting them. Some people seem to possess knowledge about the past or about places they have never visited. They can describe situations in such detail that it can only be explained as second sight.

Is it possible that an officer with second sight could have accurately predicted a bombing raid on a convoy like this one—or was it just a coincidence?

CHAPTER 2

MEDIEVAL MYSTICS

The Middle Ages in Europe lasted from about 500 CE to about 1500 CE. The period was dominated by the Catholic Church, and being a good Christian was very important in a world based on religion. The Church did not accept many traditional superstitions, such as second sight. However, many Christians claimed to have abilities that were similar to what we would now call ESP.

Some medieval Christians claimed to have visions in which they met Jesus Christ and other holy messengers.

The pope was the head of the Catholic Church. He was the most powerful man in medieval Europe. People lived their lives according to the teachings of the Church. They believed that their actions on Earth would decide whether they went to heaven or hell when they died. Some people claimed to have had visions of what heaven was like or of the tortures of hell. These people were like ancient seers, but because what they saw was related to Christian teaching, their visions were believed to come from God.

Encounters with God

There were many different sorts of medieval Christians. One small group, known as mystics, claimed to have special powers that enabled them to have personal encounters with God himself. Mystics could come from any background, but they were usually women and were often nuns. They entered a state called ecstasy, which was an altered state of consciousness like a trance or dream. In this state, mystics could see and feel things that ordinary people could not. They had visions in which God's love pierced them like arrows.

The more painful a mystic's experience was, the closer he or she was thought to be to God. The mystic's pain was seen to echo the suffering of Jesus Christ when he was crucified, or killed on the cross. Mystics were not seen as mad, but as being specially chosen by God. Their visions of an extra-sensory world were valued as signs of their great Christian faith.

Saint Teresa of Ávila, a sixteenth-century nun, claimed to feel the spirit of God enter her in a state of ecstasy.

13

CHRISTIAN SEERS

Some medieval Christians claimed God had allowed them to foretell the future, an ability called precognition. Others carried marks on their bodies that showed the suffering of Jesus Christ. The Catholic Church accepted these examples of ESP as signs of God's power. Some people who experienced them were canonized, or made saints.

King Oswald (*bottom right*) was one of a number of important medieval kings in Britain.

Foretelling Victory

Columba of Iona was an abbot and missionary who lived in Ireland in the sixth century CE. He introduced Christianity to Scotland, where he founded an abbey on the island of Iona that is in operation today. Columba claimed to be able to see the present and the future at the same time, and he accurately predicted many events. It was said that he visited King Oswald of Northumbria in a dream in 633. Oswald was preparing to go into battle against a Welsh king named Cadwallon ap Cadfan. In the dream, Columba advised Oswald when to begin his attack and promised him victory. Oswald did as he was told. When he won the battle, he and all his leading nobles converted to Christianity. Oswald came to be seen as a saint after his death in 642.

Marks of the Cross

Many centuries later, the Catholic Church canonized Padre Pio. This Italian priest from the first half of the 1900s spent 50 years with marks on his body known as stigmata. Stigmata are scars and wounds that appear in the same positions as the wounds inflicted on Jesus Christ when he was killed. There are usually marks in the palms of the hands and in the feet where nails held Jesus to the cross. Sometimes, stigmatics, as people with the marks are known, also have a wound in their left side, where Jesus was injured by a spear. Doctors who examined Padre Pio could not explain how his wounds had come about, although some said they could have been burned with acid. Padre Pio was very unusual, because stigmatics are four times more likely to be women than men.

While Padre Pio was training as a monk, one of his friends claimed to have seen him rise off the ground in a state of ecstasy.

A Visionary Nun

Anne Catherine Emmerich was a nun in Germany in the early 1800s. She claimed to see into the future and the past. She also displayed stigmata. She had wounds around her head that echoed the Crown of Thorns that Jesus wore on the cross, and her wrists and feet bled from wounds. Emmerich claimed to have visions in which she talked to Jesus Christ and the Virgin Mary. She was beatified by the Catholic Church, the first step to being made a saint, in 2004.

A FRENCH HEROINE

During the Hundred Years' War (1337–1453), England and France fought in what is now France. In the 1420s, a young peasant girl named Joan of Arc claimed to have a vision that God had chosen her to lead the French forces.

Joan was an unusual military leader. Not only was she a teenage girl at a time when men dominated society, she was also a peasant at a time when military leaders all came from the nobility. Joan was uneducated, and she had no military training. She had been brought up as a Catholic, however, and knew the church's teachings by heart.

A Mission from God

When she was just 13 years old, Joan started to hear voices. She believed God was telling her to save France by helping the crown prince Charles of Valois defeat the English. As a sign of her devotion to God, Joan took a vow never to get married.

Wars in the 1400s were fought entirely by mounted knights or by foot soldiers armed with bows or crossbows.

Into Battle

In May 1428, Joan set out on her mission to save France. She made her way to where the French army was camped near Orleans. She tried to persuade people to let her talk to the prince until eventually a noble agreed. Joan cropped her hair and wore boys' clothes to meet Charles. She promised him she would defeat the English so he could be crowned king of France. The prince was so convinced that he agreed to let Joan lead troops to Orleans, where the English had the city surrounded. Joan led the French into battle. Her bravery inspired the soldiers, who defeated the English and saved the city. Charles became King Charles VII, just as Joan had predicted.

The English captured Joan and put her on trial for heresy, or going against the teachings of the church. She was found guilty and burned at the stake in 1431, aged just 19 years old. In 1920, Joan was made a saint, and today, the French still see her as a symbol of unity and nationalism.

After her death, Joan was celebrated every year by the people of Orléans. In 1920, the Catholic Church made her a saint.

NOSTRADAMUS

In 1555, a French author and astrologer named Nostradamus published *The Prophecies*. The book has been in print more or less constantly ever since, and is thought to predict the future. People who believe that Nostradamus was able to see the future claim that he correctly foretold many world events. These included the Great Fire of London in 1666, the rise of Adolf Hitler as the leader of Germany in the 1930s, and the two world wars of the twentieth century.

A trained pharmacist, Nostradamus was also an astrologer. This meant he studied the position of the stars in the night sky to figure out what would happen on Earth. He also made predictions after having feelings and seeing visions. His first prediction was said to take place when he came across a group of monks herding cattle. He knelt down in front of one of the monks and called him "Your holiness," the title used for the pope. Years later, that monk became Pope Sextus V.

Nostradamus did not come up with all of his prophecies from scratch—he adopted some of them from earlier works.

Many Predictions

To make his words seem more learned, Nostradamus wrote in an odd mixture of French, Latin, Greek, and Italian. Many prophecies were vague sentences and riddles, which people have interpreted over time in many ways.

Some predictions that seem specific appear to have come true. Nostradamus wrote "The blood of the just will be demanded of London, burnt by the fire in the year 66...," and much of London did indeed burn down in 1666. However, most predictions have failed to happen or have not happened yet. Critics of Nostradamus say most of his words are so vague people can read into them whatever they want—which makes it easy to prove them right or wrong.

The Great Fire of London destroyed more than 13,000 homes and public buildings.

Predicting His Own Death

One prediction Nostradamus did get right was his own death. On the evening of July 1, 1566, he told his assistant that he would not see morning. He was right—he died during the night.

19

CHAPTER 3
THE POWER OF THE MIND

The seventeenth and eighteenth centuries are sometimes known as the Age of Reason. People began to look beyond the church to explain the world around them. The first scientists began to observe things closely and tried to explain what they saw. They did not accept that ESP and other paranormal events had a divine, or godly, origin. They wanted explanations based on logic and reason.

A Magic State of Mind

Two men, Dr. Franz Mesmer and the Marquis de Puységur, believed that humans could reach a state of mind that was different from the everyday world. Mesmer was a German doctor who believed living things possessed a magnetic fluid that caused disease if it was out of balance. Mesmer tried to restore the balance using Mesmerism, which was an early form of hypnotism.

Mesmer's attempts to balance the body's magnetic fluid led him to be able to unlock hidden parts of the mind.

20

Critics called Mesmer a fraud, or fake, but they agreed that he had unlocked great abilities in the brains of his subjects. Today, we know that hypnosis is an unconscious state of mind. A hypnotized person loses any power over their thoughts and actions, and responds to the instructions of another person. Hypnotism sometimes seems to give people remarkable skills or immense strength.

LAUSANNE. — GRANDE SALLE DU CASINO.

MAGNÉTISME

MARDI 9 Juin 1857, à 8 heures et quart du soir.

E. ALLIX

PROFESSEUR DE MAGNÉTISME ET MEMBRE DE PLUSIEURS SOCIÉTÉS SAVANTES

DONNERA UNE

SÉANCE DE MAGNÉTISME

dans laquelle il démontrera de la manière la plus concluante l'existence du principe MESMÉRIEN et son action sur l'organisme humain. — Outre l'attrait qu'offrent aux hommes de science les séances de M. ALLIX, elles font aussi une large part à la curiosité du public en général.

PROGRAMME

Sommeil instantané. Effets divers de paralysie, de catalepsie partielle ou complète, d'attraction partielle ou générale.

EFFETS PHRÉNO-MAGNÉTIQUES, ou confirmation du système de Gall, par la manifestation de quelques-unes des facultés cérébrales, excitées magnétiquement.

EXTASE MUSICALE, phénomène pendant lequel la surexcitation [...] leur apogée. La pupille, considérablement [...]

INSENSIBILITÉ AUX DOULEURS [...]

Afin de prouver que le sommeil [...] l'état de veille, un grand nombre de ph[...]

Transfusion de la puissance magné[...] momentanément sa propre puissance à [...]

PRIX DU [...]

This poster advertised a public display of "animal magnetism," the unseen force Mesmer believed joined all living things.

COURS DE MAGNÉTISME EN 10 LEÇONS

The Power of Hypnosis

Mesmer's realization that hypnosis could be studied scientifically, not as a form of magic, was shared by one of his followers, the French noble the Marquis de Puységur. De Puységur opened his own clinic, where he successfully treated many patients. He noticed that when his patients went into a trance, their state was similar to those of sleepwalkers. He concluded that the mind had power to perform all kinds of acts and by harnessing this power, the mind could make things happen that had previously seemed beyond the ability of the conscious mind.

ASTRAL PROJECTION

While people were starting to figure out that some unexplained phenomena were more likely explained by the abilities of human beings than by ideas about gods or magic, a craze began for what were called astral projections. Today, these are better known as out-of-body experiences, when a person feels as though they leave their body. Sometimes, they simply look down on themselves, but at other times, they travel to distant locations. Those who believe in astral projection claim that people achieve it by using their own mental powers. However, there is no scientific evidence that astral projection has ever taken place.

Out of the Body

One of the first scientists to claim to have had an out-of-body experience was the Swedish inventor and thinker Emanuel Swedenborg. After he had been rejected by a woman he loved, Swedenborg decided to put all his energies into his scientific studies. He was particularly interested in the workings of the human brain.

Emanuel Swedenborg inspired a new Christian movement, known as Swedenborgianism.

Swedenborg started to write down his dreams, which he believed must reveal something about the real nature of the world. In 1744, he dreamed he saw Christ and then God, who told him to tell the world the truth about Christian teaching. Swedenborg later claimed to have traveled to both heaven and hell in his trances. He wrote books about conversations he had with people who had died, and with angels and devils. He met spirits in his dreams and described what hell looked like—in fact, he said it appeared very similar to Earth.

A Royal Supporter

Many people thought that Swedenborg was making up his accounts of mind travel, but others believed him. Some of the things he reported seeing seemed to reflect real events. He correctly described a fire in the Swedish capital, Stockholm, in 1759, even though Swedenborg was hundreds of miles away at the time. In October 1761, the Queen of Sweden summoned him to make contact with her dead brother. She claimed that Swedenborg told her things that only her brother could know.

A Psychic Explorer

Helen Keller was born in Alabama in 1880. When she was a small child, she became deaf, mute, and blind, but her teacher, Anne Sullivan, taught her to read and write braille, which is writing that blind people feel with their fingertips. Helen went on to study languages and music at university, swim, and ride horses. She was a follower of Swedenborg and claimed that she had used astral projection to travel to Athens, in Greece. She was able to describe the famous ruins of Athens as if she had been able to see them.

25

UNDERSTANDING ESP

By the nineteenth century, there was a growing amount of research into things that could not be explained by reason or science. In the Victorian age, many people believed that ESP existed, and that there was a spirit world that most humans could not see. They said that those who could experience this world had what they called psychic powers. However, many people refused to take psychics seriously. It was, after all, impossible to prove that ESP existed because it lay beyond reason.

Despite this, in the late nineteenth century, scientists set out to prove the unprovable. In 1882, the Society for Psychical Research was founded. It was set up to conduct scientific, scholarly research into human experiences such as clairvoyance and other paranormal phenomena. The London-based society tried to carry out scientific research into the growing fashion for spiritualism, which was communicating with the dead. It also set out to challenge centuries-old religious beliefs based on the existence of heaven and hell. In the end, the society did not produce any definitive findings.

Some individuals set out to deceive. For example, these photographs from 1939 show a medium produce a "spirit" from her mouth—in fact, it is cloth.

Experimenting with ESP

It was not until 1930 that an American scientist devised a test he claimed proved the existence of ESP. Joseph Banks Rhine used special cards. Each card was printed with one of five different simple patterns: a circle, a square, a star, a plus sign, and wavy parallel lines.

For his test, Rhine put people in separate rooms. He shuffled the cards, then asked the first person to draw a card and concentrate hard while trying to project the image to the other person. The second person concentrated to see if he or she could receive any message, then tried to choose the correct card. There was a one-in-five chance of getting the right card by simple guesswork, so Rhine argued that any success higher than that showed that the second person possessed ESP. The more cards they got right, the stronger their ESP.

Some of the test subjects matched nearly all the cards. Years later, however, one of Rhine's assistants claimed that the results had been faked. and that even the most successful subjects were simply guessing which card had been turned over. He said that even the best results were based on coincidence, not special powers.

The Zener cards were designed by the US psychologist Karl Zener, who worked with Rhine at Duke University.

CHAPTER 4

SPIRITS AND SÉANCES

Between 1840 and 1920, spiritualism was a great fashion in the United States and Great Britain. People held séances and consulted mediums, who claimed they could talk to the dead or spirits. Although scientists argued that there was no evidence for the existence of spirits, some mediums became great celebrities.

Contacting the dead through séances was particularly popular with the wealthy, who often hired mediums.

A Victorian Craze

The Victorian craze for spiritualism began in 1848 in New York State. Two sisters, 11-year-old Kate Fox and 14-year-old Margaret claimed to have contacted a ghost who haunted their family home and answered questions using a simple system of taps to mean yes or no. Word spread of the girls' ability, and soon they were performing in front of large audiences. Spiritualism as a form of public entertainment had been born.

Frauds and Fakes

Spiritualism was an easy target for fraud. For all the mediums who did seem to contact the dead, the same number simply pretended so they could take money from those desperate to have contact with their beloved dead. Even when the Fox sisters admitted in 1888 that they had made up their knocking ghost, millions of people continued to believe that it was possible to contact the dead. They included the creator of Sherlock Holmes, Sir Arthur Conan Doyle, who believed completely in the spirit world. Today, many people still believe in spiritualism and consult mediums.

Consulting the Spirits

By the end of the nineteenth century, more than 8 million people believed in spiritualism. They thought that the spirits of the dead survived in the "spirit world" and could communicate with the living. It gave people comfort to hear from their dead friends and relatives. Additionally, because the spirits were thought to be better qualified than the living to give advice, many people turned to them for guidance. There was a dramatic rise in the popularity of spiritualism after World War I (1914–1918), when millions of people lost relatives in the conflict.

Some mediums were eager to trick people into believing they could contact dead relatives.

A PRESIDENT'S DREAM

On April 14, 1865, shortly after the Civil War (1861–1865) had ended, President Abraham Lincoln visited Ford's Theater in Washington, DC. While he watched a play with his wife, he was shot in the head by an assassin, or murderer. Lincoln died the following day from his wounds.

Whose Body Is It?

Lincoln was the first president to be murdered—and the first president to foretell his own death. Just three days before the murder, Lincoln had a powerful dream in which he saw his own funeral. He described how he was in the White House in his dream and could hear wailing. He wandered around, trying to find the source of the noise. When he entered the East Room, he saw a body lying on display with its face covered. The body was guarded by soldiers. The president asked who the guards were protecting, and they told him it was the body of the president, who had been killed by an assassin.

Abraham Lincoln was shot by John Wilkes Booth, who had supported the Confederacy in the Civil War.

On the day of his murder, people noticed that Lincoln looked happier than he had for months. His wife took this as a sign that something bad was about to happen.

A Voyage

The president had told his cabinet about another dream he said he had before every major battle of the Civil War, including Gettysburg. In this dream, Lincoln said he was onboard a vessel he could not describe as it moved "toward a dark and indefinite shore." Some people think this was a description of the journey to the afterworld.

After his death, Lincoln's body was taken by train to Oak Ridge Cemetery in Springfield, Illinois.

Talking to the Dead

In 1862, Abraham Lincoln's son Willie died at the age of 12 after catching a disease from drinking dirty water. Lincoln and his wife, Mary Todd Lincoln, were heartbroken. Mary had to stay in bed for three weeks. She later organized several séances at the White House, during which a medium tried to make contact with Willie. The president also attended these séances. At the time, many people believed mediums could contact the dead.

29

DON'T SAIL ON THE SHIP

On April 10, 1912, the RMS *Titanic* set sail from Southampton in England bound for New York on its maiden, or first, voyage across the Atlantic Ocean. Its passenger list was full of the rich and famous. The ship used the very latest technology. Its builders said it was unsinkable. Four days later, the *Titanic* hit an iceberg. Within three hours, the unsinkable ship had sunk. Of the 2,208 passengers and crew, 1,503 died.

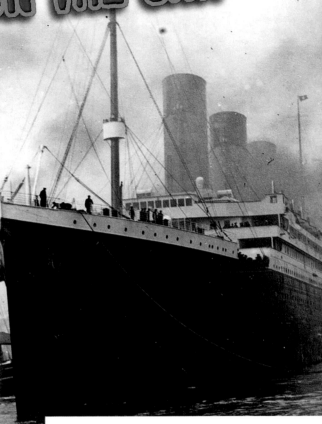

When the *Titanic* left Southampton, many passengers believed they were traveling on the safest ship afloat.

Bad Feelings

Some of those on board predicted a disaster. They had a feeling they could not explain that something bad was going to happen. Their worries were recorded in letters they wrote while on board. The ship's Chief Officer, Henry Tingle Wilde, wrote to his sister, "I still don't like this Ship. I have a queer feeling about it." He did not survive. One survivor, seven-year-old Eva Hart, later claimed that her mother did not sleep on the ship because she was convinced something bad was going to happen.

Canceled Trips

One couple named Mr. and Mrs. Bill had a lucky escape when they decided not to sail on the *Titanic* at all. Mrs. Bill said she had a premonition that the *Titanic* would sink, so they changed their tickets. They sailed to New York on a ship named the *Celtic* instead. One of the most famous people to decide not to sail and to change his booking was George Washington Vanderbilt. He was the grandson of the shipping and railroad businessman Cornelius Vanderbilt, one of America's richest men. Vanderbilt and his wife canceled their first-class tickets for the *Titanic* at the last minute. Nobody knows why—but one story is that a family member had a premonition about the ship and warned the couple not to sail.

Many passengers survived the sinking of the *Titanic* in lifeboats, but there were not enough for all.

A Tragic Tale

One of the most startling predictions of the *Titanic* disaster had been made years earlier. In 1898, a writer named Morgan Robertson wrote a a short novel called *The Wreck of the Titan*. It told the story of a doomed Atlantic liner named the *Titan*, which is very similar to *Titanic*. Like the *Titanic*, the *Titan* is the largest ship afloat, and its makers say that it is unsinkable. Eerily similar to the *Titanic*, the *Titan* hits an iceberg and sinks. Also like the *Titanic*, the *Titan* does not have enough lifeboats to hold all the passengers on board.

CHAPTER 5

PREDICTING TRAGEDY

Despite the scientific advances of the twentieth century, and growing doubts about the paranormal, the public appetite for ESP remained high. From horoscopes that told people their futures to the rise of TV psychics such as Uri Geller, people continued to place their faith in the paranormal.

Daily Horoscopes

Newspaper horoscopes owe their existence to Great Britain's Princess Margaret, the Queen's younger sister. In 1930, after Margaret's birth, the British astrologer R. H. Naylor wrote her horoscope for a newspaper. He predicted Margaret's life would be eventful. The horoscope was so popular, the newspaper asked him to write more. One horoscope he wrote predicted danger to a British aircraft. Soon afterward, a British airship crashed in Paris, killing 48 people.

The zodiac is a circle based on the yearly path of the sun through the sky. It is divided into 12 signs.

After the prediciton of the airship crash, everybody started to take notic of horoscopes. Naylor then created a horoscope based on the signs of the zodiac for people with birthdays that fell within a particular week. Within a few years, he was writing daily predictions for all 12 signs of the Zodiac. Today, millions of people still read their horoscopes in newspapers and magazines. According to one 2009 poll, 26 percent of Americans believe in astrology, which is the idea that the movements of heavenly bodies influence life on Earth.

Bending Spoons

During the 1970s, the Israeli magician and psychic Uri Geller wowed TV audiences in the United States and Great Britain with his ability to control events using his mind. One of his favorite tricks was to bend metal spoons. Many people did not believe in Geller's skills, but he was a popular entertainer. In the same way, even in an age of scientific reason and technological advances, many people still believe in fortune telling methods such as using Tarot cards. Psychics and mediums are still kept busy today.

Uri Geller created a spoon-bending craze when he appeared to do so by rubbing them lightly with a finger.

DEADLY TRAGEDY

In October 1966, after days of heavy rains, a large pile of waste from a coal mine slipped and covered an elementary school in the small town of Aberfan in Wales. More than 140 children and teachers were killed in the disaster, which stunned Great Britain.

Shortly after the disaster, many people came forward who claimed to have predicted it, usually in a dream. A psychiatrist named John Barker was contacted by more than 60 people who said they knew the disaster was going to happen. It was also claimed that some of the victims of the disaster themselves had felt that something was going to happen.

The black area in the center left of this picture is the waste slip. The school is circled.

Victims and Survivors

One victim was 10-year-old Eryl Mai Jones, a student at the school. Two days before the disaster, she told her mother she was not afraid of dying because she would be with her friends, Peter and June. She said she had dreamed that she went to school, but there was nothing there, because something black had covered everything. Eryl was killed in the disaster, along with her friends Peter and June. They were buried side-by-side—just as Eryl predicted.

In Plymouth, on the English coast far from Aberfan, a housewife also dreamed about the disaster before it happened. In her dream, she clearly saw a boy who was saved from the school. She told her friends at church about her strange dream. When the effort to rescue children from the ruined school was shown on TV, she recognized the boy from her dream among the survivors from the destruction.

Death of a President

Jeane Dixon was the leading twentieth-century clairvoyant in the United States. Among other predictions she made that came true was the assassination of John F. Kennedy. In 1956, Dixon predicted in her magazine column that the upcoming 1960 presidential election would be won by a Democrat—but that the winner would either be assassinated or die in office. She was proved right when Kennedy was shot dead in Dallas, Texas, on November 22, 1963. Dixon also correctly predicted the Apollo disaster of 1967, when three astronauts died in a fire during a rocket test.

This image of John F. Kennedy (*left*) was taken minutes before he was shot.

CLAIRVOYANCE OR COINCIDENCE?

People who believe in the paranormal see evidence of it everywhere. They point to predictions that have come true from sources that range from the sixteenth-century French seer Nostradamus to episodes of the popular animated TV series *The Simpsons*. Some people believe the TV show predicted the terrorist attacks of 9/11. This, they argue, proves that it is possible to predict the future. Other people argue that what they see as predictions are nothing more than coincidences.

Predicting a President

In 2000, *The Simpsons* apparently predicted that Donald Trump would become president, which he did at the start of 2017. In 2000, Trump was a businessman who was known for slightly odd statements about public events. *The Simpsons*' episode referred to "President Trump," but the show's writers say this was not clairvoyance. They just thought it was a funny way to point out changes taking place in US society and politics.

Predicting the Attacks

Another prediction apparently made by *The Simpsons* is more difficult to explain. The 1997 episode "The City of New York vs Homer Simpson" shows a magazine advertisement for a $9 bus ride to New York City. The figure "9" is next to the Twin Towers of the World Trade Center. The towers resemble the number 11, so the image looks as if it reads 9/11.

On September 11, 2001 (9/11), terrorists flew hijacked airliners into the Twin Towers, killing thousands of people. It was the worst terrorist attack in US history. No one on *The Simpsons* had any explanation for how they had come up with the 9/11 frame. The writers of the show said it was a coincidence— but some people still claim that it was somehow a prediction of the future.

A Vision of Technology

Some people point out that it is not very difficult to predict aspects of the future. This is particularly true of science, where even unlikely ideas from science fiction sometimes become real. In 1900, for example, the engineer John Elfreth Watkins wrote an article in *Ladies' Journal* magazine, predicting what might happen in the next century. His predictions included the invention of the TV and of cell phones. Watkins was no clairvoyant, however. He simply took his experience of engineering and thought about what might one day be possible.

Smoke rises after the first airliner struck the Twin Towers on 9/11. Another airliner struck the second tower shortly afterward.

37

CHAPTER 6

PSYCHIC CONTROL

Today, ESP has become part of the entertainment business. While millions of people claim to believe in ESP, many of its practices have been debunked, or disproved, by research. This has not kept TV psychics from successfully creating million-dollar careers.

A police technician photographs a crime scene. The medium Allison DuBois claimed to be able to help solve such crimes by contacting the spirits of victims.

Solving Crimes

Medium was a popular TV drama that ran from 2005 to 2011. It featured a character who used her psychic powers to help the police solve crimes. The series was fictional, but it was based on the book *Don't Kiss them Goodbye* (2004) by Allison DuBois. DuBois describes herself as a medium and profiler, and the book chronicled her psychic experiences. After becoming a lawyer, DuBois began to "see" crimes, leading her to discover hidden clues and even to lead the police to hidden bodies.

TV Careers

Another medium who has had a successful TV and writing career is Theresa Caputo, star of the show *Long Island Medium*. Caputo claims that her psychic gift allows her to pass messages from the dead to the living. Like Caputo, the TV personality John Edward claims to have realized as a teenager that he had a psychic gift. He claims to put people in touch with dead relatives.

Sceptics claim that such mediums prey on vulnerable people. A retired magician named James Randi has made it his business to prove that TV psychics are fakes. In 1996 he created the One Million Dollar Paranormal Challenge. He offered one million dollars to anyone who could demonstrate any paranormal, supernatural, or occult power under test conditions. In 2015, he ended the challenge because nobody would accept it, including John Edward.

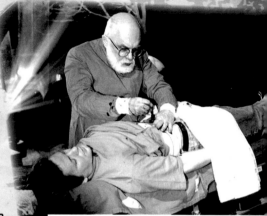

James Randi pretends to carry out "psychic surgery" on TV to show that it is a hoax.

A Surgical Hoax

Some people claim to be able to carry out surgery with their bare hands, using a technique called psychic surgery. They identify diseased organs by laying their hands on the body, then seem to push their hands through the skin to remove infected tissue. They leave no wound, which they claim heals at once. James Randi showed how the procedure can be staged using animal parts, fake blood, and magic tricks.

THE COLD WAR

During the Cold War, a struggle for global influence between the United States and the Soviet Union that began in the 1950s, research into the paranormal became part of military planning. When a Russian woman claimed to be able to move objects with her mind, US politicians were eager to avoid an "ESP gap" opening between the United States and its enemies.

Following World War II (1939–1945), the US government began to explore ways it could control and influence human behavior. Using ESP and other paranormal tactics became part of government planning. Various federal agencies researched anything that might unlock people's psychic powers and give them special gifts. For example, they tested eating special mushrooms that made the mind act in odd ways.

During the Cold War, the two sides pointed thousands of missiles at one another—but the United States was eager to use ESP as a weapon, too.

Mind Control

In the 1960s, a woman named Ninel Kulagina appeared on Russian TV and seemed to move objects with her mind. Whether it was real or not, the US government was alarmed. It ordered the Department of Defense to investigate the "Soviet pyschoenergetic threat." Pyschoenergetic refers to energy produced by the mind. During the Cold War, the United States was terrified that the Soviets might gain any kind of advantage in any area, including the paranormal. The government was then willing to ask scientists to investigate even unlikely topics of research.

The government's interest in the paranormal and psychics continued for the rest of the twentieth century. In 1988, the Department of Defense used a psychic to try and locate a US Marine who had been kidnapped by a terrorist group named Hezbollah in the Middle East. The psychic claimed that the Marine was still alive in Lebanon and being moved frequently. In fact, it later turned out that he was already dead.

Psychic Dogs

One of the strangest parts of the US Army Cold War research came in 1952. The Army asked Duke University to test whether dogs were psychic. Researchers carried out 48 tests to see if dogs could locate underwater explosives. At first, researchers decided the dogs were psychic, because they were able to locate explosives they could not have known existed. It was then pointed out that a dog's sense of smell is 50 times greater than humans and that their hearing is four times as good, even underwater. Discovering the explosives was the result of remarkable skills—but it had nothing to do with ESP.

41

REMOTE VIEWING

The Stargate Project was the name given to a secret US Army unit set up in 1978 to investigate the possible military use of psychic abilities. Its main focus was on remote viewing—the ability to use the mind to see a remote or hidden target from a different location.

The Mind as a Weapon

A small unit of between 15 and 20 individuals based at Fort Meade, Maryland, had the job of remotely "seeing" distant events and people. The inspiration for the unit came from the US government's worry that the Soviet Union had its own psychics. Army scientists tested psychics to see if they could help. One of their candidates was the Israeli Uri Geller. He was later judged to be a complete fraud after he was interviewed by the University of Oregon psychology professor, Ray Hyman.

Conflicts such as the Korean War (1950–1953) convinced US military planners to explore the use of psychic weapons.

Still No Proof

The Stargate Project remained open until 1995. When it was closed down, a report on its activities concluded that it had not been able to confirm that it was possible for a person to perceive a remote or hidden target.

The Stargate Project cost $20 million. It had access to the latest technology and best scientists. Despite that, however, it was unable to find any proof that ESP and the paranormal exist. Yet it seems that many people are just as willing to believe in them now as they were among our ancient ancestors.

Staring at Goats

The idea of using mind control as a weapon is not new. In the 1950s, a small unit of special forces soldiers based at Fort Bragg in North Carolina are supposed to have practiced their psychic powers on a group of goats at the "Goat Lab" medical training facility. The goats' ability to bleat had been removed, so the tests could take place in secret. According to reports, one special forces sergeant was able to kill a goat just by staring at it. The soldiers became known as "the men who stare at goats"—but no one knows for sure whether they even existed.

Some people think the whole "Goat Lab" story is a hoax.

43

TIMELINE

633 — St. Columba visits King Oswald of Northumberland in a dream to promise him a military victory.

1428 — Inspired by a religious vision, Joan of Arc leads French soldiers to victory over the English at Orléans.

1555 — Nostradamus publishes *The Prophecies*, a famous collection of predictions about the future.

1567 — St. Teresa of Ávila writes an account of witnessing the presence of God during a state of ecstasy.

1666 — Fire destroys much of London, as predicted by Nostradamus.

1744 — Swedish scientist Emanuel Swedenborg begins to have his first visions of God.

1779 — Franz Mesmer develops techniques based on "animal magnetism" that gain access to hidden parts of the mind.

1848 — Kate and Margaret Fox begin a craze for spiritualism in the United States.

1865 — Abraham Lincoln dreams of his own funeral three days before he is killed.

1882 — The Society for Psychical Research is founded to find evidence of ESP.

1912 The *Titanic* sinks on its first voyage; some people claim to have foreseen the disaster.

1918 The Italian monk Padre Pio displays the first signs of the stigmata.

1930 The first modern horoscope is created for the British princess Margaret.

1934 The work of psychologist Joseph Banks Rhine starts to make the phrase "extra sensory perception" widely known.

1952 Researchers at Duke University test whether dogs might be psychic.

1956 US medium Jeane Dixon predicts the assassination of the next president, which comes in 1963.

1966 More than 60 people claim to have predicted the Aberfan disaster in south Wales.

1978 The US government begins the Stargate Project to develop remote viewing and other psychic techniques for military use.

1997 *The Simpsons* animated TV show seems to predict the terrorist attacks that take place on September 11, 2001.

2015 After 20 years, James Randi ends his One Million Dollar Paranormal Challenge after no one proves the paranormal exists.

GLOSSARY

astral Related to a non-physical type of existence.

astrologer Someone who studies the stars to find out what will happen.

coincidence Events that seem to be connected but are not.

Cold War A period from the 1950s to 1980s when the United States and the Soviet Union competed for global influence.

consciousness A person's awareness of something.

convoy A group of vehicles or ships traveling together.

fairy A small, imaginary being with magical powers.

folk stories Tales that are handed down from one generation to the next.

foretell To predict a future event.

go-between Someone who passes messages between two people.

hoax A deception.

horoscopes Forecasts of people's futures based on the stars and planets.

hypnotism The act of putting someone into a trance.

interpreted Explained the meaning of something.

logic A process of thinking according to strict laws of reason.

mystics People who seek a magical experience of God.

nationalism A belief in the importance of one's country.

occult Mystical and magical events and powers.

perception Being aware of something through the senses.

phenomena Things that exist and can be experienced.

predicted Forecast what would happen in the future.

premonition A strong feeling that something bad is about to happen.

prophecies Predictions of the future.

psychic surgery Surgery carried out without cutting the body.

reason Thinking in a logical way.

remote Far away.

rituals Religious ceremonies.

sacrifice Something given to the gods.

sceptics People who do not believe something.

science fiction Stories based on imagined scientific advances.

séances Meetings to try to contact the dead.

seers People who see the future.

sensory Related to the senses.

shrine A holy place.

special forces Elite, highly trained military personnel.

spiritualism A belief that it is possible to communicate with the dead.

supernatural Not explained by science or the laws of nature.

superstitious Having beliefs that are not based on reason.

unconscious Part of the mind that acts without conscious thought.

visions Seeing things that do not really exist.

vow A solemn promise.

witches People thought to have magical powers.

FOR FURTHER READING

BOOKS

Klepeis, Alicia. *ESP, Superhuman Abilities, and Unexplained Powers* (Paranormal Investigations). New York, NY: Cavendish Square Publishing, 2017.

Maurer, Tracy Nelson. *Eerie ESP* (Fear Fest). Minneapolis, MN: Lerner Publications, 2017.

Nagelhout, Ryan. *The Prophecies of Nostradamus* (History's Mysteries). New York, NY: Gareth Stevens Publishing, 2015.

Small, Cathleen. *The Science of Mind Control and Telepathy* (Science of Superpowers). New York, NY: Cavendish Square Publishing, 2018.

WEBSITES

ESP—*science.howstuffworks.com/science-vs-myth /extrasensory-perceptions/esp.htm*
This website explains what makes some people believe in ESP —and why some people still do not believe.

Nostradamus—*www.biography.com/people/nostradamus-9425407*
Discover facts about the life and predictions of Nostradamus.

Oracles—*greece.mrdonn.org/greekgods/oracles.html*
Learn about Apollo's oracle at Delphi.

Spiritualism—*www.bbc.co.uk/religion/religions/spiritualism /history/history.shtml*
Read all about the history of modern spiritualism.

Publisher's note to educators and parents: Our editors have carefully reviewed these websites to ensure that they are suitable for students. Many websites change frequently, however, and we cannot guarantee that a site's future contents will continue to meet our high standards of quality and educational value. Be advised that students should be closely supervised whenever they access the Internet.

INDEX